315 PRAYER BULLETS THAT GUARANTEES INSTANT RESULT

PRAYER THAT DISMANTLES SATANIC SPELLS DESTROYS WITCHRAFT MANIPULATIONS AND GUARANTEES ALL ROUND BREAKTHROUGH

Vin C. Butcher

Copyright © Vin C Butcher

2017

All rights reserved

No portion of this book may be used in any way without the written permission of the publisher

E-mail: vincentbutcher@gmail.com

Unless otherwise indicated, all Scripture quotations are taken from the King James Version of the Holy Bible.

TABLE OF CONTENTS

Contents

TABLE OF CONTENTS..................................3

HOW TO USE THIS BOOK............................4

INTRODUCTION..5

PRAYER BULETS...6

HOW TO USE THIS BOOK

This prayer bullets are effective with when used by a child of God. Everybody on the earth is not children of God.

'Ye are of your father the devil, and the lusts of your father ye will do. he was a murderer from the beginning, and abide not in the truth, because there is no truth in him. When he speaketh a lie, he speaks of his own: for he is a liar, and the

father of it.' John 8:44

Being a child of God is by choice. So I want to lead you to Christ before we proceed so that this prayer bullet will be a blessing to you.

Say after me,

Lord Jesus, I come to you as a sinner. I know I am a sinner that cant help myself. I give my life to you, wash me with the blood of Jesus Christ, give me the power to become a child of God. Thank you for doing it.

After you have done this, feed your spirit always with the Word of God

This prayer from the stand of victory, have strong faith

These prayer bullets will be more effective in the night period.

'Another parable put he forth unto them, saying, The kingdom of heaven is likened unto a man who sowed good seed in his field:

25 But while men slept, his enemy came and sowed tares among the wheat, and went his way.' Matt 13:24

Most demonic atrocities are perpetuated in the night. Pause and ponder on this. Why do most attacks on humanity happen in the night? According to the above scripture, it is when men sleep that the devil (the enemy) attacks.

This prayer bullet is meant to scatter whatever the enemies have done against you, your family, your business.

Start the prayer by midnight.

Start with singing worship songs; worship brings down the presence of God at least for 45 minutes.

Begin to thank God for His goodness,

call Him sweet names as you are led

Pray for mercy for your self and your family using Psalm 51

Invite the presence of the Holy Spirit and the Angels of God.

Pray against the spirit of fear.

Then, start praying with the prayer bullet with anger in your spirit, pray with desperation.

Pray each prayer bullet for at least 5mins

Use only ten prayer bullets per session

The prayer bullets can be repeated because the potency doesn't expire

INTRODUCTION

This book is a compilation of proven, and result oriented prayer bullets that will guarantee your freedom from the dominion of the powers of darkness, and guarantee your freedom.

The disciples of Jesus asked Him.

'And it came to pass, that, as He was praying in a certain place, when he ceased, one of his disciples said unto Him, Lord, teach us to pray, as John also taught his disciples.

2 And he said unto them, When ye pray, say, Our Father which art in heaven, Hallowed be thy name. Thy kingdom come. Thy will be done, as in heaven, so in earth.' Luke 11:1-2

Jesus also gave a prayer guide to His disciples, which we call today 'The Lord's prayer.' He gave them a guide on how to pray.

This book is to give you a guide on how to fight against the powers of darkness that attacks you through many mediums.

PRAYER BULLETS

1. My Father, I praise Your Holy name for bearing my burden on a daily basis, I thank You for You are the Refiner, I thank You for the greatness of Your works, I thank thee for You are the sun of righteousness in Jesus name.

2. God, I thank You for You are a great God and King over all gods, I thank You for being my Physician in Jesus name.

3. Great Father of Glory, I thank You, because in Your hand is the depths of the whole earth and the mountain peaks belong to You in Jesus name.

4. My Father, I thank You for You are my Messiah, I thank You, for the marvelous things that You have done for me, I thank You, for being my Prophet. I thank You for redeeming my life from the pit and for crowning me with compassion and love in Jesus name.

5. Lord, I thank thee for being the strength of my soul. I thank You for satisfying my desires with good things so that my strength is renewed like the eagles in Jesus name.

6. God my Father I thank You for being my Cornerstone. I thank You for making the cloud Your chariots and for riding on the wings of the wind. Heavenly Father, glory be to Your Holy name, for making the winds Your messengers and Your minister's flames of holy fire in Jesus name.

7. My Father, I thank thee for being the Bishop of my Soul in Jesus name.

8. Dear Holy Spirit, come down upon me and incubate my life afresh, in the name of Jesus Christ.

9. Every anti-repentant spirit in my life, I bind you and cast you now, in the name of Jesus Christ.

10. Let my steps be withdrawn from every wickedness, in the name of Jesus Christ.

11. I refuse to become a companion of sin, in the name of Jesus Christ.

12. My Father, empty me of selfishness, in the name of Jesus Christ.

13. Lord, heal every area of backsliding in my spiritual life, in the name of Jesus Christ.

14. Oh Lord, restore unto me the joy of salvation, in the name of Jesus Christ.

15. Lord, anoint my head with fresh oil, in the name of Jesus Christ.

16. Oh Lord My Father, cast me not away from thy presence, in the name of Jesus Christ.

17. Thank You Father for the power and the benefits, provision of the Blood of Jesus Christ. Thank You because the blood of Jesus has secured my freedom from every satanic bondage. I plead the blood of Jesus to wash, cleanse, purify my spirit, soul, and body now from every filthiness, pollution, contamination and every sin I have committed in the mighty name of Jesus Christ.

18. I stand on the ground of the Blood of Jesus Christ to proclaim victory over sin, Satan and his agents and the world, and I command every waster, oppressors, destiny hijackers, Luciferian farmers, poverty activators and problem expanders working against my destiny to be disgraced and frustrated now by the blood of Jesus Christ in the name of Jesus Christ.

19. I apply the Blood of Jesus Christ to every stubborn problem, evil circumstances, and challenges in my life, in the name of Jesus Christ.

20. I plead the Blood of Jesus Christ from the top of my head to the sole of my feet, in Jesus name.

21. I soak my entire life in the Blood of Jesus Christ, in Jesus name.

22. I paralyze all satanic oppressions delegated to me by the Blood of Jesus Christ.

23. Let all doors that I have opened to the enemies be closed forever by the Blood of Jesus Christ.

24. Through the Blood of Jesus Christ my Lord, I have been redeemed out of the hands of the devil and his evil kingdom of darkness in Jesus name.

25. I walk in the light, and the Blood of Jesus Christ cleanses me from all sins in Jesus name.

26. Through the Blood of Jesus Christ, I am justified, sanctified and made holy with God's holiness in Jesus name.

27. Through the Blood of Jesus Christ my Lord, I have the life of God in me in Jesus name.

28. Through the Blood of Jesus Christ my Lord, I have access to the presence of the Lord in Jesus name.

29. I paralyzed and cut off the head of my Goliath by the Blood of Jesus Christ.

30. If there is anything in my life that is not of God, I don't want it. Depart, in the name of Jesus Christ.

31. Let the Blood on the Cross stand between me and any dark power delegated to me, in Jesus name.

32. I curse all works of darkness in my life to dry to the roots by the Blood of Jesus Christ.

33. I defeat, paralyze and overthrow the spirit of demotion, failure at the edge of a miracle, financial downgrading, inherited problems, vision killers, dream attackers, marital problems, by the roots by the Blood of Jesus Christ.

34. Let all the powers of the Blood of Jesus Christ be released on my behalf now! And let it speak now against every dead bone in my life, in the name of Jesus Christ.

35. Blood of Jesus Christ be released on my behalf now and let it speak against every demonic and stubborn mountain in my life, in the name of Jesus Christ.

36. Witchcraft battle assigned to disgrace me, downgrade my destiny, make my life difficult and problematic, am not

your candidate, what are you still waiting for, die, in the name of Jesus Christ.

37. Powers that defeated my parents, and is still fighting to defeat me, hear the word of the Lord, my case is different, die suddenly without remedy, in the name of Jesus Christ.

38. Battles assigned to my life on my day of glory, am not your candidate, scatter beyond redemption, in Jesus name.

39. Every negative monitoring power from my foundation and in this city which I now dwell, die, in the name of Jesus Christ.

40. Environmental witchcraft assigned to my progress, ministry, career, marriage, finances, health, business, spiritual life, scatter, in Jesus name.

41. Generational battles against my destiny, hear the word of the Lord, Jesus Christ has purchased my victory on the cross; therefore, die, in the name of Jesus Christ.

42. Thunders of darkness that pursued my parents, and is still pursuing me today, my life is different now, die, in Jesus name.

43. Let every strange leg that has walked into my life to introduce struggles, delays, disappointment, failure at the edge of miracles and breakthrough, walk out by fire, in Jesus name.

44. Garments of inherited battles, problems, crisis, failure, setback, oppression, affliction, sickness and poverty, projected upon my life from my foundation, from my father's side

and mother's side catch fire, in Jesus name.

45. Every power that would want to attack me, fall down and die, in Jesus name.

46. Strongmen behind my battles, die, in the name of Jesus Christ.

47. Strongmen behind my problems, die, in the name of Jesus Christ.

48. Witchcraft wars against me and my household, backfire, in the name of Jesus Christ.

49. Internal enemy pretending to be friends and carries my matter to the coven of darkness; you are a liar; die suddenly without remedy, in Jesus name.

50. Hard battles programmed from my foundation, the habitation of cruelty,

marine kingdom, expire in the name of Jesus Christ.

51. Every power prolonging my battles in life in every department of my life, what are you still waiting for, die, in Jesus name.

52. Altars of darkness in my foundation and in this city which I now dwell, let me depart by fire, in the name of Jesus Christ.

53. Any power that does not want me live and enjoy the full blessings which Jesus death on the cross was meant to achieve for humanity especially those that know God, die, in Jesus name.

54. I recover my breakthroughs, miracles, blessings, wealth, gifts, glory, benefits, virtues and all that

legitimately belongs to me from the warehouse of the enemy, in Jesus name.

55. Any power circulating my name for evil, misfortune, calamity, untimely death, destruction, oppression, afflictions, problematic life, impossibility, failures, financial hardship, marital instability, retardation, ministerial and career failure, in all the realm of darkness, expire, in the name of Jesus Christ.

56. Covens of darkness assigned to destroy me and any member of my household, properties, blessings, wealth, career, scatter beyond redemption, in Jesus name.

57. Any object used to represent me in the coven of darkness, catch fire in Jesus name.

58. Covens of darkness in my place of birth manipulating my destiny and sponsoring any problem affecting my destiny today, scatter in Jesus name.

59. Afflictions, reproach, trouble of any kind from the coven of darkness targeted at me and my household, we are not your candidate, therefore, backfire in Jesus name.

60. Any coven in my habitation, my dwelling place, place of worship, go now by fire, in the mighty name of Jesus Christ.

61. Every personality standing as my wife/husband in the coven of darkness be burnt to ashes in Jesus name.

62. Any document assigned to move my life forward, bring me promotion,

breakthrough, honor, greatness, success in life that has been captured by the coven of darkness, be released in Jesus name.

63. My money, or anything that belongs to me in the coven of darkness, and the custody of the strong man, the evil powers of my fathers, mother's house be released by fire in Jesus name.

64. I use this money and others personal effects as a magnet to recover my wealth from the coven of darkness, in the name of Jesus Christ.

65. Arrows of poverty, confusion, depression, fear, infirmity, stagnation, demonic manipulation from covens of darkness directed against my destiny and household, backfire in Jesus name.

66. Every demonic bank manager assigned against me from the coven of darkness in my foundation and in this city which I now dwell, what are you still waiting for, die suddenly without remedy, in Jesus name.

67. O God, arise in Your fierce anger and let the covens of darkness assigned to me and my household scatter in Jesus name.

68. Every power planning my untimely death, accident of any kind, problems that waste money, and my name in covens of darkness, you are a failure, die in Jesus name.

69. Witchcraft agenda, embargo, curses, spells, enchantment, and divination against my destiny, household, what are you still waiting for, scatter in the name of Jesus Christ.

70. Every Prince of Nigeria in my life, the fire of God, consume it now in Jesus name.

71. Every spiritually crude and morally senseless ideology that is offensive to the scripture projected into my life from the habitation of cruelty, evil altars, die by fire in Jesus name.

72. Every spirit of antichrist spirit in me, and in my habitation, place of work, I chase you out by fire, in Jesus name.

73. Every information about me and my household, I cover with them with the blood of Jesus Christ.

74. Every evil foundation of my father's house, I destroy you by the Holy Ghost fire. I reconstruct another foundation for myself, my generation

on Christ the Solid Rock, in the name of Jesus Christ.

75. Every evil foundation of my mother's house, I disassociate myself and my generation from you. I re-erect a brand new foundation laid on the Lord Jesus Christ of Nazareth in Jesus name.

76. Every negative effect of my foundation on my life and the life of any member of my household, be broken by fire in Jesus name.

77. Any bondage that the former foundation has put me in, I come out by fire in Jesus name.

78. Every covenant of eternal damnation in hellfire, I reject you in Jesus name.

79. Father, reveal to me anything in my family foundation that is negatively affecting me and members of my household today in Jesus name.

80. Every family spirit that has walked with my ancestors that wants to continue its evil works in my generation, I am not your candidate, my case is different, therefore, die by fire in Jesus name.

81. I decree that every evil yoke that I am carrying because of my foundation, I reject the yoke henceforth in Jesus name.

82. Every evil pattern in the lineage, I break and stop your work in Jesus name.

83. Every covenant of death and hell arising from my foundation be destroyed by fire in Jesus name.

84. Any age, long spot of failure in which the power of my father's house, mothers have tied me down, Holy Ghost fire go there and release me by fire in Jesus name.

85. Every tool of the wicked ones used to reprogram my destiny, jump out by fire in Jesus name.

86. Every confirmed demon, selected demon, familiar demon, associated demon, ancestral demon, relationship demon, programmed demon, experienced demon in charge of my family problems, die by fire in Jesus name.

87. Every evil altar in my father's house having my name, in a triangle, I command the sword of the Lord to locate you for destruction now in Jesus name.

88. The satanic altar that is used to cause sorrow, discomfort against my family, be destroyed by fire in Jesus name.

89. Every gunshot from Astra witches that has brought poverty and other traces of failure in my life, dissolve by fire in Jesus name.

90. Any of my blessings that I have lost through food in the dream or the physical, I recover it from marine caterers in Jesus name.

91. Every bondage that is tying my life down to a spot be broken by fire in Jesus name.

92. I disconnect myself from every evil inherited curses by fire in Jesus name.

93. The rod to deal with Pharaoh of my foundation, come into my hands, in the name of Jesus Christ.

94. Every covenant made by my father or my mother with Satan, die, in the name of Jesus Christ.

95. Every anti-breakthrough altar raised against my life, die, in Jesus name.

96. Every evil altar raised against my life, carry your judgment back to the sender, in Jesus name.

97. Evil fetish power rising against me, pursue your owner, in Jesus name.

98. Every power speaking judgment to my breakthroughs, shut up and die, in the name of Jesus Christ.

99. Every strange contact that has followed my life, break away, in Jesus name.

100. Evil arrows fired against me, backfire and locate your sender, in Jesus name.

101. The storm of the wicked shall not find me, in the name of Jesus Christ.

102. I separate my life from violent death and destruction, in the name of Jesus Christ.

103. I shall receive uncommon breakthroughs and promotion in

every area of my life now, in Jesus name.

104. I claim divine peculiarity. I must shine, in the name of Jesus Christ.

105. I will not build my destiny on witchcraft and marine spirit, occultic foundations, in Jesus name.

106. I bind every unprofitable investment in my life, in the name of Jesus Christ.

107. The hand of the enemy will not prevail against me nor any member of my household, in Jesus name.

108. Thou contrary king reigning in my destiny, I dethrone you and enthrone Jesus Christ, therefore die, in Jesus name.

109. The hand that smite Herod to death smite my oppressors, devourers, destiny manipulators, witches and wizards, and evil powers of my father's house in Jesus name.

110. Thou power of the tree, road junction and marketplace working against my destiny and my family, die, in Jesus name.

111. After the order Moses, I raise my staff of prayer to divide my Red Sea, in Jesus name.

112. Oh Lord, release sufficient plagues to disgrace my Pharaoh in my foundation, in the name of Jesus Christ.

113. My God my Father that sitteth in the heavens laughs my oppressor's

enemies to scorn, in the name of Jesus Christ.

114. Thou conscious and unconscious covenants with marine power, spirit husband/wife break by the blood of Jesus, in Jesus name.

115. Arrows of affliction, reproach and adversity, bondage and captivity, come out of my body, in Jesus name.

116. Thou curse of affliction, emptiness, stagnation, demotion, confusion, depression, fear, worry, poverty, financial insolvency, die in the name of Jesus Christ.

117. I break down every witchcraft pot over my life, in Jesus name.

118. Every council of witchcraft working against me will not prosper, in Jesus name.

119. I release myself and my family members from every witchcraft cage and pot, in Jesus name.

120. I retrieve my integrity from the hands of household witchcraft, in Jesus name.

121. O Lord, let the eyes of witches monitoring my life be darkened, in Jesus name.

122. O Lord, let the covens of witchcraft become desolate, let there be no one to dwell in them, in the name of Jesus Christ.

123. Every plantation of death, die, in the name of Jesus Christ.

124. Every witchcraft of hand, planting evil seeds in my life through attacks in the dream, wither and burn to ashes, in Jesus name.

125. All the friendly witchcraft powers, be exposed and disgraced now, in the name of Jesus Christ.

126. O Lord, plant your warring angels around me, to dismantle and destroy evil stronghold of internal witchcraft, in the name of Jesus Christ.

127. I exercise my authority over stubborn witchcraft powers and I pull down its structures, in Jesus name.

128. Every witchcraft plan, targeted at my destiny, what are you waiting for? Die, in Jesus name.

129. Placenta witchcraft, manipulating my destiny, die, in Jesus name.

130. Every blessing that I have lost through placenta witchcraft, I repossess you, in Jesus name.

131. I command the crash landing of witches and wizards assigned against my breakthrough, in the name of Jesus Christ.

132. I command the sun to smite on my oppressors in the day, and the moon and the stars to smite them at night time, in the name of Jesus.

133. Every stronghold of death on my mind and imagination be pulled down, in the name of Jesus Christ.

134. I programme divine health, divine favor, long life, spiritual

advancement into my life by the power in the blood of Jesus Christ.

135. I shall never die, but live, to declare the works of God Almighty, in the name of Jesus.

136. I command every witchcraft coven and marine bank, release my placenta, in Jesus name.

137. Every cage of family witchcraft, release my breakthroughs, in Jesus name.

138. My Father, my Father, let signs and wonders be my lot, in the name of Jesus Christ.

139. All the obstacles in my life, give way to miracles now, in the name of Jesus Christ.

140. I command every frustration in my life, become a bridge to my miracles, in the name of Jesus Christ.

141. I held the blood of Jesus against every satanic delay to my miracles, breakthroughs in the name of Jesus Christ.

142. I decree by fire, thunder and brimstone that I shall not die before the manifestation of my miracles and glory, in Jesus name.

143. You miracle evil hijackers, release my miracles now by fire and thunder, in the name of Jesus Christ.

144. Every harmful spiritual deposit in my life, I command you to catch fire now, in the name of Jesus.

145. O Lord God, arise and speak healing and creative miracles into my life, in Jesus name.

146. My entire organs receive creative miracles, in the name of Jesus.

147. My Father my Father, arise by your signs and wonders and visit my life, in the name of Jesus.

148. O God of wonders, Like the rising of the sun, arise now in my life, in the name of Jesus.

149. O Lord God of signs and wonders, heavenly Surgeon, touch me by your power, in the name of Jesus.

150. O Lord, let the wonder-working power of God be released to my situation for signs and wonders, in the name of Jesus Christ.

151. Signs and wonders and miracles appear in my life, in the name of Jesus Christ.

152. Holy Ghost fire, visit me with your signs and wonders, in Jesus name.

153. O Lord God, arise and hear me in the day of trouble, in the name of Jesus Christ.

154. O Lord my God, I run into your name that is a strong tower, saves me, in the name of Jesus Christ.

155. O Lord, my God let all my stubborn problems be buried, in the name of Jesus.

156. I shall not die because of of the weight of my problems, in the name of Jesus.

157. I shall never be disgraced because of my problems, in the name of Jesus.

158. Fire of God, begin to attack all miracle hijackers assigned against my life, in the name of Jesus.

159. The Lord has made me a product of His possibility; no good thing shall be impossible for me, in the name of Jesus Christ.

160. Let every curse and covenant of impossibility over my life, break, in the name of Jesus Christ.

161. Oh you Goliath of impossibility in my life, die, in Jesus name.

162. I shall not die undiscovered, in Jesus name.

163. I shall not die unused and without being celebrated in Jesus name.

164. I shall not die uncelebrated and unmissed, in Jesus name.

165. I shall never die unfruitful and unfulfilled in Jesus name.

166. Every good thing the enemy has swallowed in my life, be vomited, in Jesus name.

167. O God my God, arise, send me help from the sanctuary and strengthen me, in Jesus name.

168. O Lord, let my rescue and deliverance be announced from heaven, in Jesus name.

169. I command that before I finish praying these prayers, O Lord God, let your angels move into action on my behalf, in Jesus name.

170. Every Prince of Persia and all rullers of darkness that are hindering God's miracle in my life, scatter, in the name of Jesus Christ.

171. I bind and cast out of my vicinity, all prayer and miracle blockers, in Jesus name.

172. You miracle hijackers terrorizing my life, release my miracles now, by fire, in the name of Jesus Christ.

173. Every satanic umbrella that is preventing the heavenly showers of blessings from falling on me, catch fire, in the name of Jesus Christ.

174. Oh Lord God, arise and let my heavens open right now, in the name of Jesus Christ.

175. I shall never give up, because I believe that I must see the goodness of the Lord God my Saviour in the land of the living, in Jesus name.

176. O Lord, let my soul be prevented from death, my eyes from tears and my feet from falling, in Jesus name.

177. Everybody will hear my testimonies and glorify the name of God in my life, in the name of Jesus Christ.

178. My Father my Father, let your divine intervention in my life bring souls to the, your kingdom, in the name of Jesus Christ.

179. I use the blood of Jesus Christ my Lord to fight and defeat every spirit of impossibility in my life, in the name of Jesus Christ.

180. I release myself from the evil captivity of impossibility, in the name of Jesus Christ.

181. Every evil seed, every evil root and all tentacle of impossibility in my life, die, in the name of Jesus Christ.

182. I withdraw my name and everything concerning my life from the altar of impossibility, in the name of Jesus Christ.

183. I reject to swim in the ocean of impossibilities, in the name of Jesus Christ.

184. Every King Uzziah making it impossible for me to see the glory of God, die, in Jesus name.

185. The wind of impossibilities shall not blow in my direction, in the name of Jesus Christ.

186. You river of impossibility flowing near and around me, dry up now, in Jesus name.

187. I receive the strength of the Lord to leap over the wall of impossibility, in the name of Jesus Christ.

188. Every Red Sea of impossibilities, part, in the name of Jesus Christ.

189. You angels of possibility and success, begin to minister unto me, in Jesus name.

190. With the Lord God on my side, no good thing shall be impossible for me, in Jesus name.

191. I will reach my goals in life before my enemies know what is happening, in Jesus name.

192. I shall fulfill my destiny in this life, whether the enemy like it or not, in the name of Jesus Christ.

193. Evry of my steps shall be ordered by the Lord Almighty to fulfill my destiny, in the name of Jesus Christ.

194. O Lord, let my disgrace be turned into grace, in the name of Jesus Christ.

195. O Lord, let the dry bones of my destiny, come alive, in the name of Jesus Christ.

196. Henceforth, in my life, I embark on a journey into destiny accomplishments in all ramifications, in the name of Jesus Christ.

197. I cut off by fire the spiritual umbilical cord through which evil flows into my destiny, in the name of Jesus Christ

198. No evil word spoken from the sun, moon and stars will prosper in my life, in Jesus name.

199. Every evil word of incantation and chanting from prayer mats, evil forests, sacred trees, road junctions, major marine environment and occult prayer houses, be silenced, in the name of Jesus Christ.

200. Father, thank You for a change in my situation, in the name of Jesus Christ.

201. Every power of darkness that needs to die for my testimony to manifest, die, in Jesus Christ.

202. Every agenda of the enemy mocking powers for my life, backfire, in the name of Jesus Christ.

203. By the power in the blood of Jesus Christ of Nazareth, I receive the miracles that will puuut my friends in suprise and shock my enemies, in the name of Jesus Christ.

204. Dark authorities sponsoring continuous and repeated problems, scatter, in the name of Jesus Christ.

205. By the superpower that divided the Red Sea, let my way open, in the name of Jesus Christ.

206. By the power that caused the stone, that smote the forehead of Goliath to kill him, let the stubborn problems die, in the name of Jesus Christ.

207. By the power that divided River Jordan, let my unusual breakthroughs manifest, in the name of Jesus Christ.

208. By the power that disgraced Sennacherib, let evil covens gathered against me catch fire, in the name of Jesus Christ.

209. Every evil power mocking my prayers, receive double destruction, in the name of Jesus Christ.

210. O God of Elijah, arise and make me a mysterious wonder, in the name of Jesus Christ.

211. Oh Lord by the word of God which cannot be broken, I move into my next level, in the name of Jesus Christ.

212. Every satanic priest working against my breakthroughs, be disgraced, in the name of Jesus Christ.

213. My season of unusual laughter and victory dance, manifest, in the name of Jesus Christ.

214. I commnd that whatever has tied down my destiny, break lose from my life, in the name of Jesus Christ.

215. Witches toying with my destiny be wiped off, in the name of Jesus Christ.

216. O Lord! Reshuffle my environment to favour me, in Jesus name.

217. I will be a champion and not a casualty, in the name of Jesus Christ.

218. If I have been disconnected from my destiny, O God, arise and re-connect me to it, in the name of Jesus Christ.

219. O Lord my God, whatever you have not positioned into my life, wipe it off, in Jesus name.

220. Oh Lord my God, dismantle the poison in my foundation, in the name of Jesus Christ.

221. Every circumstance affecting my success, bow, in the name of Jesus Christ.

222. Oh Lord God, arise and give me a strong reason to celebrate and laugh this year, in Jesus name.

223. All my enemy shall weep concerning my life this year, in the name of Jesus Christ.

224. My Father, show me unusual secrets about my next level, in the name of Jesus Christ.

All the months of this year shall be a disappointment to the enemy, in Jesus name.

225. My father my Father, distract my enemies with problems that are bigger than they, in the name of Jesus Christ.

226. Oh Lord God, arise and make my star shine, in the name of Jesus Christ.

227. My adversaries hear the word of the Lord" "carry your loads", in the name of Jesus Christ.

228. Every evil serpent assigned to bite my destiny, die, in the name of Jesus Christ.

229. Oh Lord God, arise and fight for me in the day and in the night, in the valley and on the mountain, in the name of Jesus Christ.

230. Every power assigned to scatter my resources, dry up, in the name of Jesus Christ.

231. Every evil power assigned to suppress my elevation, die, in the name of Jesus Christ.

232. Every satanic panel set up against me, scatter, in the name of Jesus Christ.

233. You rod Rod of the wicked attacking my progress, break, in Jesus name.

234. Delayed breakthroughs, delayed promotions, manifest by fire, in Jesus name.

235. I disarm all lingering problems, in the name of Jesus Christ.

236. I disgrace all discouraging powers, in the name of Jesus Christ.

237. O Lord God, arise and give my enemies leanness this year, in the name of Jesus Christ.

238. You my enemies will not rejoice over me this year, in the name of Jesus Christ.

239. I decree that sorrow and tears, I uproot you from my life by fire, in the name of Jesus Christ.

240. Any evil power assigned to sink the boat of my salvation, die, in the name of Jesus Christ.

241. Every arrow of pain and sickness, go back to your sender, in the name of Jesus Christ.

242. Every arrow of weakness and disease, go back to your sender, in the name of Jesus Christ,

243. Let every effort of the enemy to weaken my prayer altar, be frustrated, in the name of Jesus Christ.

244. Every unclean spirit assigned to be molesting me in the dreams, die, in the name of Jesus Christ.

245. Every spirit spouse assigned to be polluting my body in the dreams, die, in the name of Jesus Christ.

246. Let the thunder and the lightning of God blind every spirit spouse, in the name of Jesus Christ.

247. Let every spirit of immorality, wickedness and witchcraft manifesting in the form of dogs and serpents appearing in my dreams die in the name of Jesus Christ.

248. I barricade my life and home with the fire of God against the operations of spirit spouses and let the finger of God unseat my household strongman, in Jesus name.

249. Every power using my dreams to hold back my progress in life, die, in the name of Jesus Christ.

250. Whatever concoction I have been fed with as a child, I vomit in the name of Jesus Christ.

251. I smash and remove completely all the gate of hell shutting out my blessings, in the name of Jesus Christ.

252. I chase away all spirits of anxiety, worry and impatience, in the name of Jesus Christ.

253. I destroy completly all evil thoughts and imaginations against me and my household, in the name of Jesus Christ.

254. I frustrate the spirit of loneliness, I bind every spirit intimidating me, in the name of Jesus Christ.

255. I snatch by fire all the keys to my success in life and multiple

breakthroughs, in the hands of my enemies, in the name of Jesus Christ.

256. I break my covenants with familiar spirits; I break my covenants with false prophets, in the name of Jesus Christ.

257. I refuse to die young; I shall reach my full age, in the name of Jesus Christ.

258. I reject the spirit of anger, envy and jealousy. I defeat the spirit of hatred, in the name of Jesus Christ.

259. I smash all demonic mirrors to pieces and I declare that i shall not die untimely in Jesus name but live, I reject the spirit of death, in the name of Jesus Christ.

260. All demonic incisions or marks on my body, wiped off, by the blood of

Jesus. I destroy all sacrifices made on my behalf, in the name of Jesus Christ.

261. I command all those collaborating with evil forces against me be roasted by fire of God, in the name of Jesus Christ.

262. Any dark power trying to attack me to get promotion, fall down and die, in Jesus name.

263. Let my name be removed from the lists and books of failure, backwardness and poverty, in the name of Jesus Christ.

264. Demons cannot drink my blood, for it is anointed with the power of the Holy Spirit, in the name of Jesus Christ.

265. Every arrow of sorrow and mourning, fired against my life, backfire, in Jesus name.

266. Lord, convert any pain in my life to gain, in the name of Jesus Christ.

267. Oh Lord my Father, give me my personal Pentecost. Every damaged organ in my body be repaired by fire, in the name of Jesus Christ.

268. Any evil attached to my name against my blessings, be cut off and die. Every power that does not want to see me around, fall down and die, in the name of Jesus Christ.

269. I withdraw my breakthroughs and success from every evil altar, in the name of Jesus Christ.

270. Oh God, arise with all your weapons of war and fight my battles for me, in the name of Jesus Christ.

271. Every generational covenant, strengthening suffering and sorrow in my family line, be broken, in the name of Jesus Christ.

272. Lord Jesus, walk back into my foundation and carry out every reconstruction that will move my life forward in Jesus name.

273. Oh Lord God, pass through the camp of my enemies with affliction and drain their anointing of wickedness, in the name of Jesus Christ.

274. I call down the judgment of God upon every dark power assigned to donate my life, in the name of Jesus Christ.

275. Let the wicked that are oppressing me destroy themselves, in the name of Jesus Christ.

276. My portion, you shall not be mistakenly carried away with the wind. Every good and perfect thing I touch will prosper and become a harvest, in the name of Jesus Christ.

277. O Lord, let heavens break my yoke, offload satanic burdens from me by fire, in the name of Jesus Christ.

278. Every stubborn yokes assigned to my life, fall away, in the name of Jesus Christ.

279. Affliction from the dragon, break away. Every evil shadows enveloping my life, clear away, in the name of Jesus Christ.

280. Jesus Christ, the Son of God, come into my family. Everything thing the enemy has stolen from my life, I recover them, in Jesus name.

281. Every evil power attending meeting daily for my sake, I chain you to your place of meeting with the fire of the Holy Ghost, in the name of Jesus Christ.

282. I silence the mouth of the devourer. I command my destiny, jump out of every evil control, in the name of Jesus Christ.

283. Any devilish visitation in my dreams that has wasted my possession, die, in the name of Jesus Christ.

284. Oh thou wind of God, drive away every power of the ungodly rising

against my destiny, in the name of Jesus Christ.

285. I command all the rage of the wicked against me be rendered impotent, in the name of Jesus Christ.

286. I command the imaginations of the wicked against me be neutralized, in the name of Jesus Christ.

287. I command every counsel of evil kings against me, be scattered. Every cord of darkness militating against my breakthroughs, die, in the name of Jesus Christ.

288. Oh Lord God, arise and speak in great wrath against the enemy of my breakthroughs, in the name of Jesus Christ.

289. O Oh Lord God, arise and laugh my enemies to scorn, be my glory and the lifter of my head, in Jesus name.

290. I will not be afraid of ten thousand of people that have set themselves against me, in the name of Jesus Christ.

291. Lead me, O Lord, in thy righteousness, Let all my enemies gathered aagainst me be ashamed and sore vexed, in the name of Jesus Christ.

292. Let every pit dug by the enemy return upon his own head, in the name of Jesus Christ.

293. Oh Lord God, ordain strength for me and still the enemy and the avenger, in the name of Jesus Christ.

294. Arise Oh Lord God, let not man prevail, let the heathen be judged in thy sight, in Jesus name.

295. Put the enemies in fear, O Lord, that the nations may know themselves to be but men, in the name of Jesus Christ.

296. Let the mischief of all my enemies return upon his own head, in the name of Jesus Christ.

297. O Lord rain snares Upon the wicked, fire and brimstone and a horrible tempest, in the name of Jesus Christ.

298. My enemies shall not rejoice over me. Keep me as the apple of thy eye; hide me under the shadow of thy wings, O Lord, in the name of Jesus Christ.

299. Let the smoke go out of your nostril and fire out of your holy mouth to devour all plantations of darkness in my life, in Jesus name.

300. Every power of familiar spirit and witchcraft working against my mind, release me now, in the name of Jesus Christ.

301. I frustrate every demonic arrest over my mind, in the name of Jesus Christ.

302. Holy Ghost fire, destroy every satanic plantation in my mind, in Jesus precious name.

303. Every spirit withstanding testimony in my life now I bind you now in Jesus name.

304. Every river of backwardness flowing into my mind, dry up, in Jesus name.

305. Every evil association with un-friendly friends, break now, in Jesus name.

306. I destroy anything representing me in any demonic meeting, in Jesus name.

307. I break out of every internal prison in the name of Jesus Christ.

308. I arise and shine by the power in the blood of Jesus.

309. Every embargo of the enemy upon my spiritual upliftment, die, in the name of Jesus Christ.

310. You owner of evil load in my life, carry your load and die, in the name of Jesus Christ.

311. Every power of bewitchment upon my marital peace, die, in the name of Jesus Christ.

312. My life, you shall not be patterned on any satanic culture in the name of Jesus Christ.

313. I decree that any spiritual trap set for me will catch their owners in Jesus name.

314. I unseat every wrong driver from the car of my life, in the name of Jesus Christ.

VIN C. BU

Printed in Great Britain
by Amazon